A Classic Analys

The FUTURIST School
of the Book of Revelation

FAKE NEWS

*How it became a Cloak of Deception to
link the Oxford and Brethren Movements*

by

Rev. DUNCAN McDOUGALL M.A.

THE COVENANT PUBLISHING CO. LTD.
121, Low Etherley, Bishop Auckland, Co. Durham, DL14 0HA

2021

Association of Covenant People 1962
O.F.P.M. Publishers in 1970
First Expanded and Annotated Edition 1970
First Revised Edition, Lord's Covenant Church (LCC) 1982
This Edition with permission of LCC 2021

© THE COVENANT PUBLISHING COMPANY LIMITED

All rights reserved. No part of this publication may be produced in any material form (including photocopying it or storing it in any medium by electronic means and whether or not transiently or incidentally to some other use of this publication) without the written permission of the copyright owner except in accordance with the provisions of the Copyright, Designs and Patents Act 1988 or under terms of a licence issued by the Copyright Licensing Agency Ltd, 6-10 Kirby Street, London, England, EC1N 8TS. Applications for the copyright owner's written permission to reproduce any part of this publication should be addressed to The Covenant Publishing Company Limited.

ISBN 978-085205-135-1

Printed by
THE COVENANT PUBLISHING COMPANY LIMITED
121, Low Etherley, Bishop Auckland,
Co. Durham, DL14 0HA
www.covpub.co.uk

This scholarly document traces the centuries-long agenda and strategy of the Jesuits to sidetrack the Protestant Reformation. The author exposes their attempt to conceal the Historicist Interpretation of the Book of Revelation and, subsequently, God's great plan for His *Continuing* Kingdom on Earth.

The Publishers

CONTENTS

	Page
Introduction to this Edition	6
Foreword to the First Revised Edition	8
About the Author	12
Prophecy and Its Fulfilment	13
The Historicist Interpretation	14
The Praeterist Theory	15
The Futurist Theory	15
Bridging the Gulf	17
The Tractarian Movement	33
Another Fish on the Hook	35
The Oxford Movement	38
The Brethren Movement	42
The Hour and the Man	55
Darby and the "Secret Rapture"	59
Notes	72

INTRODUCTION TO THIS EDITION

The doctrines of the Futurist School of prophetic interpretation have been one of the great hindrances to a correct understanding of prophecy. They have completely blinded hundreds of thousands of men and women to the purpose and manner of God's dealings with His people Israel as separate and distinct from Judah. The teachings of this school of thought rest upon an erroneous interpretation of certain passages in the Scriptures. In order to avoid detection, the advocates of Futurism have, through skilful spiritualization, gravely misled those who have failed to investigate their assertions and properly evaluate their contentions.

The very foundation upon which the Futurists rest their case has been shown to be absolutely unscriptural. Those who have accepted this erroneous teaching have done so, in many instances, because of the vaunted academic standing of its advocates. They have failed to recognize that the scholarly attainments of individuals, or the prestige of schools of learning, no matter how high, cannot truthfully be adduced to support a doctrine, merely by sponsoring it, when factual evidence is non-existent.

From the Foreword by Howard B. Rand LL.B. to
Some Errors of Futurism, Destiny Publishers, 1936

Right up to the epoch of the Reformation, the Church fathers recognized the fact that a true understanding of prophecy lies in the acceptance of the hermeneutics of the Historicist School of prophetic exegesis, whose premise is this: *prophecy is history foretold and history is prophecy fulfilled.* There are no historical gaps in the process of fulfilment.

Like the Renaissance, which preceded it, and the French Revolution, which followed it, the Protestant Reformation was one of the three great revolutionary issues which changed the course of history. Society in the 16th and 17th centuries was agitated to its profoundest depths by this great religious insurrection. It convulsed nations with warfare and, incidentally, was a contributing factor in the colonization of America. It was a revolt against the authority of the Church of Rome as reason asserted itself and men strove for freedom of thought and worship.

As a result of the invention of the printing press, the Bible became the "little book open" (*Revelation* 10:2) during the 15th and 16th centuries and came into the hands of the common people. It became an Open Book to them and they eagerly received its message. This resulted in an awakening on the part of thousands to the realization that the Church of Rome is the "harlot" of the 17th chapter of the Book of Revelation and brought about a spiritual awakening that broke the religious shackles binding the people to Rome.

From *A Strong Delusion* by Howard B. Rand LL.B.,
Destiny Publishers, 1980

FOREWORD TO THE FIRST REVISED EDITION

This First Revised Edition of Duncan McDougall's *Rapture of the Saints* with notes has long been indicated. For at least three reasons:
1. A rising interest and increased demand.
2. The abysmal depths of prophetic ignorance, sceptical apathy and supercilious sophistication to which Protestants have been led by their leaders since the Reformation, through the Jesuit Error of a Future Antichrist, which makes a documented investigation of the facts imperative.
3. To spearhead a fresh effort to pierce the thick layer of complacency which enwraps our so-called Protestant leaders like fuzz on a cocoon. A complacency, by the way, engendered by a secret self-admission of their own remarkable qualities to see into the future, and which turns this apocalyptic business of prophetic warnings to the Saints into something akin to a picnic, a game of tiddlywinks or musical chairs. It must be stopped! Prophecy study is not a game, for serious teachers of many generations long have understood it to contain warnings to the Church-Age Saints of danger and tribulation before the Rapture – not after. Logic, a commodity which is scarce in the halls of Futurism, demands that we realize that warnings applicable to denizens of the world who have been removed from the world during an event called "Rapture" become, automatically, null and void and impotent, due to the fact that the persons to be warned have mysteriously vanished from the theatre of trouble and danger.

The great obstacle to the acceptance of the truths in this book will lie in the tendency of readers to bridle or become resentful at what they think are libellous criticisms of undoubtedly faithful and honourable men of God, a few of whom are mentioned by name in this work.

For instance: J. Wyrtzen, O. Greene, O. Roberts and many other gospellers. Our hats are off to their sincere endeavour in presenting the Gospel of Jesus Christ and His Salvation to a sin-degraded world. Even if their combined efforts resulted in the saving of only one sinner, the pointer on the scales indicates a positive quantity and the angels in heaven have been made joyous. And that, dear friend, is quite probably more than either of us has done!

But, dear critic, dear young Bible students under the thumb of some dogmatic teacher of Romanist-tainted Bible Prophecy, please listen.

You do not hire a butcher to build you a house, nor a boilermaker to repair your wife's wristwatch, do you? Why then get upset when people point to you that your favourite Gospel Preacher is a dud in the Prophecy Department?

Instead of sitting there with your mouth agape and eyes popping as he tells you of dire events to come in the Future, why not resolve to go right home to prove them. The Bereans, you know, did not trust St. Paul even, but investigated him through the Scriptures. Why should you trust Wyrtzen, Graham, and others like them, when they sneak unproved prophetic statements into their stirring Gospel messages to ruin them?

"When Thou Art Converted Strengthen the Brethren"
– *Luke* 22:32

Most certainly, "the brethren" are saved if they really believe and bring forth fruits meet for repentance, but they cannot drift into a life of ease in Zion where there is nothing for them now but psalm-singing and pleasurable anticipation of floating on clouds in Heaven. There is a work to be done – souls to be saved and brethren in the faith to be strengthened even while you are seeking lost souls. If our brethren are weak we are told to strengthen them. How? Well, if they delude themselves that a raging tiger is but a harmless pussy-cat, that is a sign of weakness – of the brain or vision. Especially if they don't have sense enough to flee. Then, again, if our brethren delude themselves into thinking an idolatrous, Bible-hating Romanist is a loving ecumenical brother in Christ, that is a bad weakness! Especially if he talks back and tells you that you are offending him by telling him that that lovely old guy over in Rome is the Antichrist!

This sort of perverted prophetic vision is just what makes a weak brother! And it is an accumulation of such weak brothers that makes a **weak church**. **And weak churches, so-called Protestant ones, are just the Pope's dish**.

Moral: teach your young people the real truths of Prophecy and you will automatically ruin the Romeward Movement, and any other movement that flouts God, Law and Order. The young people of today are tomorrow's leaders. What will they be? Hippies, Black Terrorists, or Modern Torquemadas? Whatever they become, it is quite clear that, at the rate the Protestant Reformation Prophetic Knowledge is decelerating, Protestantism will have become the next political and social minority. Once more will the country awaken to the cries of malcontents to the effect that government is unkind to minorities! Only, this time, instead of Irish, Italian, Jewish, Black, or Catholic minorities, they will be Anglo-Saxon, White and Protestant. And all this because a group of befuddled Protestant leaders flouted the warnings of Bible Prophecy when it pointed out who the enemy of the "Saints" really was – the Antichrist first popularly *revealed* by the Reformation Prophets.

We pray that this New Revised Edition will be a blessing to you and your brethren.

Rev Curtis Clair Ewing & Eric C. Peters
Revision Committee

About the Author, Rev Duncan McDougall, M.A.

One of Scotland's well-known Gaelic scholars, the Reverend Duncan McDougall graduated at Edinburgh University in Latin, Greek, Hebrew and Gaelic, taking Gaelic medals, Blackie Prize and MacPherson Scholarship (twice). On leaving college he was for eleven years Examiner in Hebrew to the Free Church College, Edinburgh, in which he had taken his theological course. Posted to Holland in the First World War, Mr. McDougall had acquired a working knowledge of Dutch, and in expectation of a mission appointment in South America, which, however, did not materialize, he set himself to acquire a working knowledge of Spanish. He was therefore a linguist of very considerable repute.

A devout Christian, Mr. McDougall was ordained to the Ministry of the Free Church of Scotland, a denomination which has long been known for its firm adherence to the teaching of the Holy Scriptures and its repudiation of modernistic and higher critical views. For six years he lectured overseas, finally returning to Scotland he was appointed Minister of the Free Church in Dunoon, a post which he held until his retirement.

PROPHECY AND ITS FULFILMENT

Historical Review

Many professed "Bible Teachers" have been busy of late years in "Bible Studies," "Conventions," "revivals," religious papers, leaflets, and books, telling with an air of authority which amounts almost to a claim to Divine inspiration, all about the "secret rapture" of the saints, and what is to take place on this earth after they are gone. According to their theory the Lord is to come **secretly** for his saints: they are to be caught up (raptured) to meet Him in the air without the world knowing that anything is happening; all who are unprepared are to be left on earth in an unsaved state; then an individual known as the "Antichrist" is to make his appearance, to assume power as a world Dictator, to revive the old Roman Empire as a ten-kingdomed confederacy, and to rule over it, to make a covenant with the Jews to allow them to set up again their temple worship in Jerusalem, and at the end of three-and-a-half years to break the covenant and persecute them. After seven years Christ is to come back with His saints to destroy the Antichrist and set up His reign of a thousand years on this earth. All these things are described in as much detail as if they were actually taught in the Bible, and even some good men have got the impression that the Bible does actually contain them.

It will come as a shock to many good people to be told not only that this teaching is not in the Bible, but that it was originated by the Bible's worst enemies! If Christians would only study God's Word, coming to the Bible with an open mind, instead of coming with their heads filled with the teachings of human and fallible men whom they treat as if inspired, they would not be so readily "carried away with every wind of doctrine."

And if they would accept the teaching of Christ that "a corrupt tree cannot bring forth good fruit," or the warning given to Daniel that "none of the wicked shall understand," they would know better than to expect to get a clean bird out of a foul nest. The pity is that so many choose to remain ignorant of the nest out of which the bird has come, and so, "professing themselves to be wise," they proclaim their ignorance as it were on the house-tops. To these "blind leaders of the blind," ignorance is a Pearl of Great Price, and to offer them any enlightenment on historical facts is an attempt to rob them of their precious jewel. If any of them have ever read any of the writings of the Reformers on the subject of Prophecy, they seldom by the slightest allusion betray the fact. Being neither willing to admit nor able to refute, the wisdom of all these mighty Spirit-taught men of God, our modern Bible Teachers studiously ignore them, and speak as if they themselves were the people, and wisdom had been born with them. One would never guess from the writings of these "Bible Teachers" that any expositor existed earlier than J. N. Darby. Naturally to tell them the truth is to become their enemy.

The Historicist Interpretation

When the Bible, after being almost unknown for centuries, was suddenly made an open book at the Reformation the Reformers saw in it a full-length portrait of the great anti-Christian system known as the "Church" of Rome, with the Pope at its head. They found in the Book of *Revelation* a prophetic account of the fiery trials through which the True Church was to pass, and also of God's judgments on her enemies. They recognized the Romish system as the spiritual Babylon denounced in that prophecy, and the Pope as the Antichrist, the Man of Sin and Son of perdition. They used the prophecy as a sharp two-edged sword with which to smite the iniquitous imposture which had usurped the place of the Church of Christ. The interpretation of prophecy as a foretelling of actual history which had been and was being strikingly fulfilled, was largely blessed of God in bringing about the Reformation.

What could Rome do? She could not blot the Book of *Revelation* out of the Bible. She had to find some other meaning for the Book, which would provide her with an alibi and turn aside the accusing finger pointed at her. The Jesuits, the most unscrupulous body of men on earth, whose "moral theology" reeks of the bottomless pit, a body whom Loyola had formed specially to undo the work of the Reformation, set to work to find a meaning for the Revelation which would side-track the Protestant.[1]

The Praeterist Theory

Alcazar, a Spanish Jesuit, started the idea that the Apostle John could not possibly foretell events which were to happen hundreds of years after his own time; that he was writing merely about what was happening in his own day, and that his Antichrist was probably the Emperor Nero or some other early persecutor. This theory has been adopted by German rationalists, and finds favour with the modernists in the churches today.

The Futurist Theory

Ribera,[2] another Spanish Jesuit, went to the other extreme and propounded the theory that the whole Book of *Revelation* related to events to take place just at the time of Christ's Second Coming, and therefore still in the future. The Antichrist was to be a World-Dictator who would appear at the end of this dispensation. The Massacre of St. Bartholomew, instigated by the Jesuits, took place in 1572, and Ribera published his theory in or about 1580 so that the blood-stains had scarcely disappeared from the streets of Paris, and in the sight of God the hands of the Jesuits were still deep-dyed with the innocent blood of the Protestants of France, when they gave their theory to the world. It was published with a design to shift the odium of being the Antichrist away from the Pope who had held a festival and struck a medal in commemoration of the massacre. Ribera was not simply a disinterested lover of the Word of God, studying Prophecy for its own sake. God has testified: "None of the wicked shall understand" *Daniel* 12:10 – yet thousands of "Bible Teachers" today maintain strongly that Ribera's ideas of a future personal Antichrist is the right interpretation, and that the reformers' view of the papacy as the Antichrist is wrong.

For 250 years, from 1580 to 1830, the idea of an individual personal Antichrist to appear sometime in the future was the recognised teaching of the Church of Rome, while the belief that the reign of Antichrist extended all through the Dark Ages, from the fourth century to the Reformation, was universally held by the Protestant Churches.

BRIDGING THE GULF

The Jesuits, owing to their vicious principles and their encouragement of treachery and violence making orderly and peaceable government impossible, have been expelled sooner or later from almost every civilized country in which they have set foot; their record covers about a hundred orders issued by different governments for their expulsion. When they were expelled from Chile, Emanual Lacunza (pronounced Lacuntha), a Chilean of Spanish descent, who had become a member of the order in 1747 at the age of sixteen, and had risen to be superintendent of the Noviciates, training them zealously in the principles of Jesuitry, came and settled in the north of Italy, where he devoted the remainder of his days to writing a book entitled *The Coming of the Messiah in Glory and Majesty*. Lacunza was, of course, steeped in the current Jesuit teaching that the appearance and reign of Antichrist was still in the future and to this he added a touch of his own, namely, that in order to make room for all the events which he anticipated, at the coming of Christ there would have to be a period of time between the rapture of the saints and the actual appearance of the Messiah in His Glory. He conceived the idea that:

> "When the Lord returns from heaven to earth upon His coming forth from heaven, and much before His arrival at the earth, He will give His orders, and send forth His command as King and God omnipotent: 'with a shout (in the Vulgate *jussu* i.e. 'by the order') with the voice of the archangel, and with the trump of God.' At this voice of the Son of God, those who shall hear it, shall forthwith arise, as saith the evangelist St. John (chapter 5:25) 'those who hear shall live'."[3]

Here is the germ out of which sprang the whole theory that Christ was to come **twice**, once *for* His saints, and again some time later *with* His saints.

But Lacunza, though largely in bondage to Romish teaching, and vigorously asserting that the Book of *Revelation* "is wholly directed to the coming of the Lord," and that it did not find its accomplishment in any sense in the facts of history during the Christian dispensation – a contention in which all Futurists and Roman Catholics are agreed – was to some extent an independent thinker, and gave expression to several views which could not but be anathema to Rome! He at least hinted that the Antichrist would appear in Rome, and that he would usurp the place of the Head of the Church. He also stated plainly that the second beast of the thirteenth chapter of *Revelation* signified the priesthood, not of some false religion, but of the Church of Rome, which he regarded as the true Church. This priesthood, he believed, was to apostatize on the appearance of the Antichrist, just as the Jewish priesthood apostatized when they crucified Christ, and, owing to the supposed sanctity of their office, they would be able to seduce the vast majority of the Christian world, and would persecute the true saints of God.

But most damaging of all, from the Pope's point of view, was the fact that Lacunza ventured to call in question the teaching of his own church as to the individual personal Antichrist, with all the supernatural powers for evil which he was to exercise within his few years reign. He actually yielded the main contention of the Protestants, that the Antichrist of the Scripture was not one man, but a mighty system or body of men animated by one spirit. Speaking of the teachings of the Romish doctors on the person of the Antichrist, he refers to their ideas as "so various, so obscure, and so ill-founded," and adds:

> "Who knows but all this variety of notions may have originated in some false principle, which without design, has been looked upon, and received as true? Who knows, but all the evil may have originated in having imagined this Antichrist as a singular and individual person, and sought to accommodate to him all the general and particular things which we find in Scripture? This supposition is the thing which has rendered very many of the notices we read in the Scripture, obscure and incomprehensible, to my understanding: which has made things and notions innumerable to be imagined, which do not appear from revelation, in order to supply the place of those which do appear. This, in short, has made Antichrist to be sought; yea, and found, and with the eyes of the imagination beheld, where no Antichrist was, and at the same time, neither to be seen, nor recognized, where he actually is."[4]

The childish notion that Mussolini, or any such individual Dictator, such as the accepted Romish teaching had led men to anticipate, can fulfil the Divine predictions concerning Antichrist, was condemned by Lacunza in words which modern "Bible teachers" might well take to heart:

> "Seeing this beast (the first beast of *Revelation* 13) is by the confession of all, the Antichrist whom we look for, and seeing by this terrible and wonderful metaphor are announced so many things, so novel, so grand, and so stupendous, as about to happen in those times over all the earth, this Antichrist ought to be something infinitely

different, and incomparably greater than what a single man can be. There is no doubt that in those dark times shall be seen, now one king, now another, now many at one time in various parts of the world, cruelly persecuting the small body of Christ. But neither shall this king, nor that, nor all conjoined, be anything in reality but the horns of the beast, and the arms of Antichrist."

"If we expect to see accomplished in one man all that is said of the beast, with all that is announced to us in so many other parts of Scripture; it is much to be feared, that, all which is written will take place, and such an Antichrist not appearing, we shall be looking for him when he is already in the house. Likewise it is to be feared, that this idea which we have formed of Antichrist may prove the chief cause of the very great carelessness in which men shall be found, when the day of the Lord arrives."[5]

The Reformers had unanimously pointed to the dreadful persecutions of the Bohemians in Eastern Europe, and of the Waldenses in the West, the long-drawn-out excruciating agony, the burnings, tortures, and unspeakable atrocities committed by the brutal soldiery, of one nation after another urged on to the murderous work by a line of Popes more degraded than the most bestial of the assassins, over a period of more than three centuries, and ending in the extermination of the Bible witness just before the Reformation, as the fulfilment of the prophetic description of the sufferings of the "Two Witnesses" and their death at the hands of the beast. The Jesuit doctors had vehemently asserted that the Two Witnesses were to be two men who should appear during the reign of the Antichrist just before the coming of Christ, and they were almost unanimous in predicting that the two had never tasted death. Lacunza strenuously opposed this view, and argued at length that:

> "From the context itself, it is easy to perceive that those Two Witnesses are as far from signifying two single and individual persons, as is the beast to whom they are opposed, and which is to persecute them to the death. It is enough to read attentively what is said of these two witnesses, from the 7th verse to the 14th, in order to perceive that they are two pious and religious bodies, or, as it were, two congregations of faithful and religious ministers of God, who, filled with the Holy Spirit, and guided by Divine Providence, shall oppose themselves to the abounding iniquity . . . . These (continues the text) the beast shall furiously persecute, but God shall visibly protect them by wonderful interferences, until they shall have fulfilled the days of their prophecy, when they shall be conquered and overcome by the beast himself, with the universal applause and joy of the inhabitants of the earth."[6]

Lacunza is striking at the speculations of the theologians of his own Jesuit order; but if he had lived today and been commenting on the imaginings of our "Bible teachers," he could not have expressed himself in any other terms.

But here several pointed questions arise, which it is not so easy to answer. On a number of the main contendings of the Reformers, Lacunza appears to be deliberately giving Rome's case away to them in the most palpable manner – an attitude in which in a Jesuit must appear peculiar; yet on other aspects he zealously maintains Rome's point of view. In a word, what he does is to take the Reformer's picture and try to fit it into Rome's frame; and the two do not fit.

He agrees with the Reformers (though without giving the slightest hint that he had ever heard of their tenets or even knew of their existence):

1. That "the beast" or Antichrist is not one man, but a vast world-wide organization animated by one spirit and ruled by one official Head who was to usurp the place of the Head of the Church, and was to have his seat in Rome.

2. That the "two witnesses" are not two individuals, but two bodies of faithful ministers of God, who were to oppose the Antichrist, and were to be finally overcome by him.

How Lacunza could describe the events so accurately, and yet fail to see the very scene he was depicting, written in fire and blood across the page of history, must remain a riddle. But to the jaundiced view of the Jesuit, the martyrs were all heretics, while he who shed their blood was the "Vicar of Christ."

But he maintains with all other Romish theologians of the Ribera school:

1. That the appearance of the Antichrist and of the two witnesses, and the fulfilment of all prophecies concerning them, are still in the future.

2. That they will all be fulfilled in a very short space of time, just prior to the Second Coming of our Lord in His Glory.

And he adds a speculation of his own, the surmise that the whole career of Antichrist will be run and all these prophecies fulfilled, within a period that will elapse between Christ's setting out from heaven and issuing the command to His angels to go out for the saints, and His actual arrival at the earth with the saints.

There is an inconsistency between the two parts of Lacunza's picture, which will at once strike every logical mind. If the whole prophecy were to be fulfilled in a short space of time, it would be more reasonable to suppose that it would be carried out under the control of one man, or super-man, and that the Antichrist be an individual World Dictator. If, on the other hand, what was prophesied was to be a vast world-wide organization, opposed by the witness of two churches or bodies of Christians, reason itself would indicate that these would require some time to develop, and that the prophecy must cover a considerable period of history.

Thus Lacunza's half-way house is an untenable position. From whichever direction it is approached, the reasoning mind cannot stop there. If he could have influenced the Church of Rome to accept the view that the Antichrist was a world-power animated by one Spirit, the inexorable force of logic would compel Roman Catholics to acknowledge that history had already produced one world-power, and only one, to answer the description; in other words, Rome would be driven to accept the Protestant position. But if he could induce the Protestant world to accept the view that the Antichrist was to appear only for a few years at the end of this dispensation, logic would equally force Protestants to picture that Antichrist as an individual person, in other words Protestantism would be compelled to accept Rome's alibi. **Which of these two was Lacunza's objective?**

It stood to reason that Lacunza's book would not affect the beliefs of his own Church. It would not, it could not, be read by faithful Roman Catholics. It differed just so widely from the accepted teaching of Rome that it was certain to be placed by the Vatican on the "Index" of prohibited books as soon as it made its last appearance, and none knew it better than the author. This indeed may well have been part of his plan. But if it was not to be read by his own Church, for whom was it written? Did he expect that a book written by a Jesuit would be read and accepted by Protestants, even if it came with the commendation of having been condemned by the Pope? That is a question. Let us see.

For four centuries before the Reformation, the Church of Rome built up her pretensions on what are known as the "Decretals of Isidore,"[7] a fictitious collection of Bulls and Rescripts supposed to have been issued by the Bishops of Rome during the first three centuries of the Christian Era, showing the authority of the popes of that early age, and alleged to have been the fruit of the researches of Isidore of Seville, one of the most learned bishops of the ninth century, though only given to the world two centuries after Isidore's death. In the general ignorance that characterized the Golden Age of the Church of Rome, the Decretals were everywhere accepted as authentic, and men beheld with awe the autocratic power wielded by Peter and his immediate followers. At the Reformation the genuine history of these centuries was examined, the forgery was discovered, and the "Decretals of Isidore" exposed as the most audacious imposture ever palmed off on an unsuspecting world. But for four centuries they did their work, and Rome reaped the benefit. What Rome has done once, she always expects to be able to do again.

It may seem a hard thing to suggest that a book written as a solemn meditation on *The Coming of Messiah in Glory and Majesty* was produced with the intention of imposing on the world in the same way. Yet the facts point that way. Lacunza wrote under the name of "Rabbi Ben Ezra,"[8] supposedly a learned Jew who had accepted Christ as his Saviour and was writing with a view to the conversion of his Jewish brethren. I see some of you pricking up your ears at this. You thought I was talking to you about a complete stranger! You had never heard the name of Lacunza before, and you did not know who he was. But you have heard about "Ben Ezra" before. You have come across some Futurist writers quoting, frequently with approval, from "Ben Ezra." Only, you always thought he was a Christian Jew; you never had any idea he was a Jesuit. Exactly. That is just what Lacunza intended you should think. How else could he expect his teaching to gain a hearing, not to speak of being accepted, in the Protestant world? With Jesuit cunning and Jesuit thoroughness the cloak of the converted Jew is worn throughout the work. Even the dedicatory prayer at the opening of the book is the prayer of "Juan Josafat Ben Ezra," the converted Jew, pleading with the Almighty to use the book for the enlightenment of his Jewish brethren; and this Jewish Rabbi does not placate the priesthood when he adds in his prayer the petition that his work would "oblige the priests to shake off the dust from their Bibles," which appear "in these times to have become, to not a few of them, the most useless of all books."

We might feel impelled to throw the cloak of charity over Lacunza, and suppose that, fearing the displeasure of his own Church for his "errors," he merely wished to hide his identity under a *nom de plume*. But one has only to glance at any account of the fierce persecution of the Jews by the Church of Rome in Spain – a vivid picture of the awful sufferings inflicted on the Jews in the name of Christ is given in Dr. Grattan Guinness' *Light for the Last Days*[9] – to see that with such bitter hatred existing between the Jews and the Roman Catholics, this guise of a Jewish Rabbi was the one best suited to secure the absolute exclusion of the book from the Roman Church. Lacunza's views might be tolerated if coming from a Jesuit, for the Jesuits within the bosom of the Church were allowed to air all kinds of views; but coming from a Jewish Rabbi the book was certain to be put on the "Index" of prohibited books.

And did Lacunza really expect to reach the Jews by pretending that the author of his work was a Jewish Rabbi? It is very unlikely that he did. The Jew, even the converted Jew, has a mentality of his own, which it would be futile for any Gentile to try to impersonate and Lacunza either was ignorant of, or did not attempt to copy, the peculiar workings of the Jewish mind; he was certainly ignorant of the writings of the genuine Jewish Rabbis, which any learned Jew would have made reference to.

Moreover, the Jewish world is too compact, and the records of all its Rabbis too well known, for any fake Rabbi to go far among them without detection. The unbelieving Jews would only smile at any attempt to influence them in favour of Christianity by foisting a fictitious Jewish Rabbi upon them. It would have the opposite of the desired effect.

There remain only the Protestants, and there can be little doubt that it was for their consumption that this elaborate forgery was prepared. To get them to begin dabbling in the theory of a future Antichrist, was worth a vast amount of time and labour to the Church of Rome.

Had Lacunza lived to see his work given to the public, he might have so managed it that the world would never have discovered the secret of its authorship. That evidently was the intention. But alas, for the best laid schemes of mice and men!

Lacunza was found dead by the river-side, where he was accustomed to go for a walk, on the morning of the 17th of June, 1801. There is no record of what caused his death. His book, or rather what appears to have been an abridgement of it, was first printed in two small volumes at the Isle of Leon, of Spain, in 1812, during the short period of the Cortez, Spain's ill-starred bid for freedom. As soon as the monarchy and papacy regained power, it was suppressed. It was also placed, as might have been expected, on Rome's Index of prohibited books, and denounced as such by the Inquisition. This was the best advertisement it could have got in those days. Immediately after the extinction of the Cortez, there were formed in Spain numbers of societies of young men and women, the object of which was "to procure, and read those books expressly prohibited by the Inquisition," of which they had got a taste under the government of the Cortez. Finding the work of "Ben Ezra" mentioned in the list, they made it their business to secure copies, which they read with delight. Soon copies or extracts made their way into France, and were read by members of the Gallican Church.

In 1816, a complete edition (apparently the first complete edition) of Lacunza's work, in four volumes, was published in London by the Diplomatic Agent of the Republic of Buenos Aires. The secret of the real authorship of the work, though still hidden from the world under its disguise, must have been known to those concerned in this publication. Otherwise, how would the Diplomatic Agent of a South American Republic be interested in the work of "Rabbi Ben Ezra," a converted Jew? But, at a time when ninety-five per cent of the whole population of South America were still illiterate, when its infant republics were struggling to lift their heads out of the primordial slime of Romish depravity, and to crawl toward the cherished goal of the terra firma of civilization an important theological work by a Native Son was something for all South America to be proud of. True, the author's identity could not be divulged – as yet. Protestant England could not be trusted to give an unbiased opinion of a book known to have been written by a Jesuit. The author must go before the British public in the disguise of the converted Jewish Rabbi, as he had himself planned. When a sufficient number of the leaders of religious thought in England had committed themselves to approval of the work, or acceptance of its teaching, and it was too late for them to reverse their verdict, then would be time enough to reveal the identity of the author, and give "honour to whom honour was due."

At that time, when everything in a printer's shop: type setting, press work, folding, binding – all had to be done by hand and the output of books in London was but a mere fraction of what it is today, the production of a theological work in Spanish, in four volumes, was an important undertaking, liable to attract much attention. Though Spanish is a simple language, one of the simplest in Europe to master, the number of people in England who would be qualified to read this work was necessarily limited; the number of copies required would be small, and the cost per set correspondingly high. Today, a copy of these four volumes, from an art dealer's point of view, might well be worth their weight in gold. When they were published, to possess, and be able to read the work of this wonderful Jewish Rabbi, would be quite a mark of distinction among the learned in London.

There was one library in London which could not well afford to be without a copy of the new publication, a theological library which was, and still is, second to none in England with the possible exception of the great University Libraries of Oxford and Cambridge. That was the library of the Archbishop of Canterbury maintained not for his private use only, but for the whole Church and people of England. We may be sure that if the Archbishop or his librarian did not take care to secure a copy, the Diplomatic Agent would be diplomatic enough to place a copy at their disposal. It must be available to any who wish to consult it at this centre of sacred learning.

Here then, on the library shelves of the official head of the Anglican Church, at the very heart's core of British Protestantism, we leave these four volumes. Rome has done her work well. She has drilled the hole in the Rock of Reformed Theology; she, has driven home the charge; she has laid the fuse; all is set for the blast which is to rend the Rock in pieces. How long will it be till the explosion takes place?

It may take years. But Rome has infinite patience. She is willing to wait.

It took ten years. A long time, do you say? What are ten years in the life of the Church of Rome? Ten years are not a very long time to produce a radical change in the thinking of a seasoned scholar and theologian, to get the man who had the care of these volumes so saturated with their teachings, that he was himself precipitated into authorship.

In 1826, ten years after the publication of Lacunza's work, Dr. Maitland, librarian to the Archbishop of Canterbury, startled the Protestant world with the first of a series of pamphlets on prophecy,[10] in which he propounded the theory, already taught for 250 years by the Jesuits,[11] that the whole Book of *Revelation* refers only to the

future, and is to be fulfilled in a short period at the return of Christ. Rev. E. P. Cachemaille, of Cambridge, describes these pamphlets as:
> "Energetically assailing the whole Protestant application of the symbols of the Little Horn in *Daniel* VII, and of the Apocalyptic Beast and Babylon, to the Roman Papacy and Church."[12]

And he adds:

> "The scheme he [Maitland] advocated was 'even more Futuristic than' the Jesuit Ribera's, for he supposed St. John even in the very first chapter of *Revelation* to plunge in spirit into (but see the Greek) 'the day of the Lord' as though the 'Lord's day,' spoken of in *Revelation* 1:10, could be the great epoch of the Lord's second coming and of the consummation of all things, passing over the whole Christian dispensation, without any guidance for God's Church and people, and ignoring the statements as to 'things which must shortly come to pass' in *Revelation* 1:1 and 22:6." [13]

But what Cachemaille failed to notice was that Dr. Maitland was borrowing, not from Ribera direct, but from Lacunza. This argument about "the day of the Lord" is Lacunza's. And in fairness to Dr. Maitland we must believe that he was quite unaware that he was using the ideas of a Jesuit; he could only have known the work as that of "Rabbi Ben Ezra," a converted Jew. The disguise had done its work. But the force of logic *drove Dr. Maitland back to Ribera's position about the personal Antichrist.* Having accepted the Futurist teaching that the whole Book of *Revelation* was to be fulfilled in a short period of a few years, the idea that the Antichrist was to be one individual World-Dictator followed naturally.

Seeing that Cachemaille has selected the argument of Dr. Maitland on the first chapter of *Revelation* as one point on which he seems to show some originality, we might take it as a test, and see whether the idea did not really originate with Lacunza. Listen to what Lacunza has to say on this subject:

> "This divine book is an admirable prophecy directed wholly to the times immediate upon the coming of the Lord. The title of the book shows well to what it is all directed; what is its argument, and what is its determinate end: 'The Apocalypse of Jesus Christ' – 'The Revelation of Jesus Christ.'[14]

> "This title till now has been taken only in an active sense as if it meant only a Revelation which Jesus Christ makes to another of future things. But I read these same words very often in the epistles of St. Peter and St. Paul, and never find them in an active sense, but always in a passive sense, and capable of no other than this – 'The revelation or manifestation of Jesus Christ in the great day of His second coming.' With this single exception, the word 'Revelation of Jesus Christ' always signifies the coming of the Lord, which we are expecting . . ."

> "I say that this divine book is wholly directed to the coming of the Lord . . . the very words with which, after the salutation to the Churches, the prophecy begins, carry a very sensible proof of this truth. 'Behold He cometh with

clouds; and every eye shall see Him, and they also which pierced Him; and all the kindreds of the earth shall wail because of Him. Even so, Amen!' *Revelation* 1:7."[15]

These extracts should be sufficient to dispel any reasonable doubt as to the source from whence Dr. Maitland drew his inspiration. If the most original idea he had to put forward was this one as to the first chapter of *Revelation* referring to the day of the Lord's second coming; we find that this was argued at length by "Rabbi Ben Ezra," and published in London ten years before Dr. Maitland used it. Dr. Maitland's argument bears the imprint of the master-hand of Lacunza.

THE TRACTARIAN MOVEMENT

Landslide Towards Rome

Almost immediately after the appearance of the first of Dr. Maitland's pamphlets a Mr. Burgh[16] in Ireland published a book on the Futurist Antichrist, along exactly similar lines, and evidently drawn from the same source. But other seven years were to elapse before the disintegration of Protestant Christianity would begin in earnest. These seven years were needed both in England and in Ireland for the idea to take root that the Reformers had done the papacy an injustice in regarding it as the Antichrist of Scripture; and that Rome was really a "sister church," and should be so regarded by the Protestants of Britain. In 1833 was the crucial year in which was to begin to be fulfilled the vision of the Seer of Patmos:

> "And I saw three unclean spirits like frogs *come* out of the mouth of the dragon, and out of the mouth of the beast, and out of the mouth of the false prophet; For they are the spirits of devils, working miracles *which* go forth unto the kings of the earth and of the whole world." *Revelation* 16:13-14.

Cardinal Newman[17] long afterward stated in his *Apologia*[18] that he never considered and kept July 14th, 1833 as the start of the *Tractarian Movement*.[19] Newman's work on the Arians of the Fourth century, published early in October of that year, appears to have been the first publication of the new movement for Reunion with Rome, the fore-runner of the *Tracts for the Times* which gave the movement its name. It is important to remember that date, July, 1833. Even Pusey,[20] most advanced Romanizer of all, did not join the movement till near the close of this year. The only publications preparing the minds of the people of England for a return to Rome, prior to July 1833, and which might be said to belong to the *Tractarian Movement*, were Maitland's and Burgh's pamphlets on the Future Antichrist.

It would take us too long to follow all the ramifications of the Oxford[21] or Tractarian, or, as it is now called, the Anglo-Catholic Movement – that is, Anglican in name and Romish at heart. We need only to note that Dr. Maitland's theory of a future Antichrist was one of the main weapons used in the Tractarian defence of the papacy from the charges levelled against it by the Reformers. It was part of the kindly light which "amid the encircling gloom" that clouded Newman's soul, "led him on" into the arms of the Pope. It was part of the "Faith of our fathers, holy faith," which Romish apologists are fond of pitting against the teaching of Scripture, and which Faber enshrined in a hymn which he left behind,[22] to be invoked by "Protestant" congregations when he himself, with seven of his monkish brotherhood, flopped over into the Church of Rome. The Romish monasteries and convents, confessionals, candles, incense, adoration of the host, and other ritualistic practices smuggled into the Church of England; the Society of the Holy Cross, Order of Corporate Re-Union, Confraternity of the Blessed Sacrament, and all the other paraphernalia of the Oxford Movement, still reaping its deadly harvest in the engulfing of precious souls in Rome's pit of perdition; all are the fruits of this teaching that the Antichrist is still in the Future, that the papacy is not the Antichrist but the true Vicar of Christ, and that the papal system is a sister Church and not the *Babylon of Revelation* – **and the end is not yet.**

Another Fish on the Hook

But we must go back to Lacunza. This wonderful Spanish work of "Rabbi Ben Ezra" had attracted so much attention in London that it must be translated into English. And here the slimy trail of the Jesuit branches off in another direction. The work of translation was undertaken by a young Scottish Presbyterian minister, brilliant but erratic, who had been assistant to the great Dr. Chalmers in Glasgow, and had come to London as minister of the Scots Church there. This was Edward Irving, founder of the "Irvingites,"[23] or, as they now call themselves, the *Catholic Apostolic Church*, a body whose beliefs and practices are among the most peculiar in Christendom. Some at least of these vagaries are distinctly traceable to the views Irving imbibed from Lacunza.

It is to Irving we are indebted for all that we know of Lacunza's life. In connection with his work of translation, Irving took pains to search for some information about the life of Rabbi Ben Ezra, the supposed author. The sponsors of the Spanish edition of 1816, must have thought the reputation of the book sufficiently securely established to make it safe to divulge the real authorship, for Irving was able to secure details of Lacunza's career and published them in the preface, although the work was still given out under the name of "Rabbi Ben Ezra."

Irving was more inexcusable than Dr. Maitland. He knew that he was giving to the world the teaching of a Jesuit and, with his Scottish Presbyterian training, he knew enough of the morality of the Jesuits to be aware of the suicidal folly of such an undertaking.

When Irving began his translation, or when he finished it, might not seem of much interest, but in this case, the date is of vital importance. I have not seen the original edition but it was a voluminous and expensive work and some time after it was published some parties, who like most of the Tractarians chose to remain anonymous, made an abridgement of it in order to publish a cheap popular edition which would give it a much wider circulation. Irving refused to allow this cheap Edition to be published until his own first edition was sold out. I have here a copy of this cheap edition, published in 1833, the year in which the *Tractarian Movement* began; and judging from the editor's apology for the delay in getting it out, I gather that there were some parties waiting to use it is soon as it appeared. This is significant. On the title page are the words:

> "Being an Abridgement of a work translated from the Spanish, and published in 1827."

Beneath is this wish:
> "Oh that my brethren in Christ might have the same divine satisfaction, and unwearied delight in reading, that I had in translating this wonderful work. Translator."

Thus Irving must have been absorbed in Lacunza at the very time when Dr. Maitland was busy on his pamphlet! A coincidence?

And at this very time Irving heard what he believed to be a Voice from heaven commanding him to preach the Secret Rapture of the Saints. Obeying this Voice, he began to preach that Christ was to come **twice**; first, secretly **for** His saints: then, after an interval of seven years – the reign of Antichrist – gloriously **with** His saints, to destroy Antichrist and to reign. Protestants had always believed, as taught in I *Thessalonians* 4:16-17, that the saints would be "caught up" (raptured) when Christ would appear in glory; and Irving's is commonly supposed to have been the first mention in the whole history of the Church of a **secret** rapture of the saints prior to Christ's appearing in glory.

But I have already shown where this idea originated. As the point is of such importance, let me quote again the suggestion of Lacunza, that:

> "When the Lord returns from heaven to earth upon His coming forth from heaven, and much before His arrival at the earth, He will give His orders, and send forth His command as King and God Omnipotent; which is all signified in these words: 'with a shout (in the Vulgate *jussu,* i.e. 'by the order') with the voice of the archangel, and with the trump of God.' At this voice of the Son of God, those who shall hear it, shall forthwith arise, as saith the evangelist St. John (chapter v. 25) 'those who hear shall live.'"[24]

The words: "He will give His orders, and send forth His command," in this passage, refer to the 'rapture' or gathering of the saints; and Lacunza says this is to happen 'much before His arrival at the earth,' so much before, in fact, that the whole reign of Antichrist and all the other events foretold in the Book of *Revelation*, are to take place between the rapture and Christ's arrival with His saints. This is exactly the order of events as described by Irving.

Please remember that I am quoting these words from Irving's own English translation of Lacunza's work, so that there can be no question that Irving had seen and studied this Jesuit doctrine before he gave out his own teaching on the subject.

The Oxford Movement

The *Oxford Movement* was founded on falsehood, cold-blooded and deliberate. This may seem a hard thing for me to say about the conduct of professedly Christian men. But I don't have to say it; the leaders of the Movement say it for themselves. Newman claims Clement of Alexandria as his authority for his own rule that a Christian both thinks and speaks the truth, except when careful treatment is necessary, and then, as a physician for the good of his patients, he will **lie**, or rather utter a **lie**, as the Sophists say. Ward, who became leader when Newman went over to Rome, is quoted by his own son, in his biography of his father as holding that:

> "When duties conflict, another duty may be more imperative than the duty of truthfulness."

The son says that his father expressed his rule thus:
> "Make yourself clear that you are justified in deception, and then **lie like a trooper**."

Hurrell Froude, another of the first leaders as early as 1834, referred to the whole Movement as *The Conspiracy* a term which accurately defines it. Pusey[25] describes their method as –

> "disposing of Ultra-Protestantism by a side wind, and teaching people Catholicism, without their suspecting,"

– so that –

> "they might find themselves Catholics before they were aware."

Their whole campaign was run according to that truly Jesuitic maxim stated by Newman in his *Apologia:*

"There is some kind or other of verbal misleading, which is not sin."

It might be supposed that a movement professing such a low moral standard would find little support among the clergy of the Church of England. But the movement swept England like a prairie fire. The publication of Newman's *Tracts* was like the sowing of the dragon's teeth, which immediately sprang up into a host of armed warriors. The founders of the movement were so amazed at the result that they were convinced that behind it all there must be a mighty spiritual power of which they were merely the instrument. Some of them, like the Witch of Endor, were startled by the spirit which they had aroused.

"Beloved, believe not every spirit, but try the spirits whether they are of God."

There can be no question that there was a supernatural power at work. **What was that mighty spirit power?** It is our duty to **try the spirits**. Would the Spirit of God, the God of Truth, teach the leaders of the movement to **lie**? Surely not. This must be a **lying spirit**, bringing on men

"a strong delusion, that they should *believe a lie*"

Dr. Maitland's teaching of a Future Personal Antichrist had created in the minds of those who accepted it a bitter revulsion of feeling against the Reformers, who charged the papacy with being the Antichrist, which prepared their minds for the reception of other teaching favourable to the Church of Rome. Hence the readiness with which the strong delusion took root.

As in the case of Dr. Maitland and the *Tractarians,* so in the case of Irving.[26] His obedience to the "Voice" which commanded him to preach the Secret Rapture seems to have been the signal for the loosing of a veritable deluge of "spirit manifestations" upon him and his poor deluded congregation.

The result was a fanatical outbreak which scandalized the whole Church. Led by a Mr. Robert Baxter, who is described as –

"for a time one of the most deluded men in the Church's History,"

– who gave utterance to the most extraordinary prophecies and angel communications, which were accepted as truths by the infatuated people, the congregation went from one fanatical extreme to another, till what had been a Presbyterian congregation formally applied for admission to the Church of Rome.

Cachemaille gives this further information, which sums up the whole connection of the "Secret Rapture" theory:

"Mr Robert Baxter subsequently repented deeply of his part in the impiety. Humbly confessing his sin, he separated himself wholly from the partisans of the 'fables' and published a *Narrative of the Facts.* He constantly maintained that the manifestations with which he had been connected were supernatural, but that Satan, not the Holy Spirit, was their author. This explains the features of the movement. It is notable that the whole movement including the origin of the "Secret Rapture" idea, belongs to the era when the three unclean and delusive spirits like frogs began to go forth. It would therefore be part of their work."[27]

As Irving's followers had shown such fanatical tendencies his influence would be confined to a comparatively narrow circle. This would not suit the delusive spirit who had initiated the work, and so, as in the case of Dr. Maitland, the teaching had to be passed on to a body filled with misguided zeal, who would create among the dissenting bodies the same confusion as the *Tractarians* were to create within the Anglican communion.

THE BRETHREN MOVEMENT

And so we must cross over to Ireland, to witness the formation of just such a body. In the "Brethren" movement[28] the seed sown by Lacunza was to find the most congenial soil in which to spread rapidly over the whole Protestant world.

It may surprise some of you to be told that there is anything in common between Tractarianism, with its hankering after everything Romish, and Brethrenism which appears to be a deeply spiritual and evangelical movement. I have long worked in the closest harmony with many earnest men among the Brethren, for whose sincerity and piety I have the utmost respect, and I should be sorry to give offence to any of them. But in the matter of prophecy, it cannot be denied that if you scratch a Brethren skin you will draw Tractarian blood.[29] Just try it for yourself, if you doubt my words. Suggest to any one of the Brethren that the Pope is the Antichrist, the Man of Sin and Son of Perdition, and that Rome is the Babylon of *Revelation*, the Scarlet Woman, and you will see him bridling up as if the Pope were a personal friend of his and as if he held a brief for the defence of Rome. Tractarians couldn't be more zealous in the Pope's behalf. It will be stoutly asserted, of course, that the Brethren and Tractarian movements will never come together. That may be true. It is also true that parallel straight lines will never meet, for the simple reason that they are proceeding in exactly the same direction. These two have attacked the citadel of evangelical Protestantism from opposite sides, but the effect on the citadel is largely the same in either case.

Serving-and-Waiting, the magazine of the Philadelphia School of the Bible, during 1925 ran a series of articles by Harry A. Ironside, now Dr. Ironside, pastor of the Moody Church in Chicago,[30] on *The Brethren Movement*. Dr. Ironside had been for years, nearly thirty, associated with assemblies of the "Brethren" and had access to documents and sources of information available to very few. He was therefore peculiarly fitted to present the world with an authentic account of Brethrenism, as it was and is; and as he was, and I believe still is, a sincere believer in the "Secret Rapture" theory, and appears to regard J. N. Darby as God's chosen instrument – eighteen centuries after the time of Christ – for first revealing this "precious" truth to the Church, we shall not do the Brethren much wrong in following his version.

Dr. Ironside mentions seven leaders of the first Brethren assembly formed in Dublin, and adds:

> "Of these it would seem that Edward Cronin was the chosen instrument to first affect the others."[31]

In other words, it was Cronin who started the meeting, and thus was the real founder of Brethrenism. Again I quote Ironside:

> "Mr. Cronin was a young dental student who had been brought up as a Roman Catholic, but had been graciously enlightened by the Spirit of God through personal faith in Christ and into the knowledge of peace with God through resting upon the atoning work of the Lord Jesus."[32]

Now, strange as it may seem to some, it is nevertheless true that there are, and always have been, true children of God within the Church of Rome; souls that have passed through the experience of conversion which Ironside here describes, and yet have not seen enough of the light to come out from Rome and be separate. Cronin came out of Rome, but he never came into the full light of Protestantism; he came far enough to form a half-way house – Brethrenism – combining the pietism of such Romanists as Thomas à Kempis with an instinctive dislike to many of the fruits of the Reformation. Such a half-way house could not have been founded by anyone who was in full sympathy with the battle waged by the Reformers.

As I have been accused of making a false charge on this head, I must, at the risk of being a little longer than usual, give a few points of Brethrenism.

First: Cronin adhered to the Romish definition of the word Church, as meaning one thing, and only one, namely, the whole body of the faithful, a body every member of which is a true child of God, and outside of which there is no salvation. Luther's discovery of the distinction between the visible church and the Church invisible was never understood by Cronin or his followers. Luther discovered that all the separate Churches mentioned in the New Testament were outwardly visible organisations, each and all of which contained members who were not truly born again, and therefore not members of the true body of Christ. None of these, nor all of them put together, were identical with the true Church, the mystic Body, which were invisible to the world and known to God alone. Cronin thought the wheat and tares should be separated here and now, and the mystic Body be identified as a visible organisation. In this boast of doing what the Apostles failed to accomplish, Brethrenism and Rome are unanimous. But the Brethren are more Romish than Rome herself in that they carefully avoid the New Testament use of the word Church as referring to a local congregation, knowing that to use Church in this sense would spoil their whole argument.

Second: Cronin and his followers carefully copied Rome in the exclusiveness and arrogance of its claim to "**the Church**," and even in the subtlety of the language embodying the claim. Rome arrogates to herself the title "Catholic" (Universal) but disliked the word "Roman" as that may seem to imply that she is only one of several Churches, and that there are other branches of the True Church besides herself. In the same way, Cronin and his followers avoided the use of any term that would seem to imply that there were any other Christians on earth besides themselves. Ironside apologizes for having to use even the term "Brethren" as if it were merely the name of a sect, adding:

> "They have from the first refused any name that would be distinctive or that could not be applied rightfully to all of God's people. Therefore, they speak of themselves as brethren, believers, Christians, saints, or use any other term common to all members of the body of Christ."

Just as Rome takes a name that belongs to the whole body of Christ. Anyone who likes can draw the inference that there are no believers, Christians, saints, outside the ranks of those to whom they apply the names. Sometimes it suits to draw it, and again, sometimes it does not.

Third: Cronin had all a bigoted Romanist's contempt for the Protestant "sects" and before forming a sect of his own tried to achieve the Romish ideal of "unity" by breaking down the bulwarks of Church membership and discipline which the Churches had erected for their own preservation. He claimed that having professed to be converted he had a right to sit at the Lord's Table in any and every Church in the city, without becoming a member of any. John

Calvin nearly lost his life in Geneva when he stood guard over the Lord's Table and refused to allow the Libertines to partake, claiming that it was his duty as the minister of God to judge the lives of those who made this profession, and to keep out those who were unworthy. Cronin's plan, if it had succeeded, would have broken down all such rule and discipline, giving the pastors or elders no "oversight" (I *Peter* 5:2) over the membership of the Church.

I myself have had a teacher of "Brethren" doctrine attempt to sit at the Lord's Table in my church without being a member of any Church; but let any of you try, and go in and "break bread" as they call it, in any Brethren meeting, and see how far you will get. Would they tolerate what Cronin tried to force upon the Churches? Certainly not!

Fourth: Cronin "also found growing up within himself a feeling of repugnance to a one-man ministry, for it seemed to him that there was no place for this in the New Testament Church." The spirit of the French Revolution was abroad in the world, and men everywhere were inclined to rebel against all authority in both church and state. The "true saying" of Paul that "if a man desire the office of a bishop, he desireth a good work" (I *Timothy* 3:1) would be reserved by Cronin, who apparently did not see why any man should be set apart to "labour in the Word and doctrine," and be "worthy of double honour" (I *Timothy* 5:17). The cry of "liberty, equality, fraternity" had gone forth, and who should be on a footing of perfect equality more than the disciples of Christ? Christ had said, "All ye are brethren" but there was a vast difference between the "brotherhood" of the New Testament, where some were set apart as elders to "feed the flock of God . . . taking the oversight thereof," and others were commanded to "obey them that have the rule over you," and the

"Fraternity" of the Revolution which aimed at obliterating all such distinctions. This is "the gainsaying of Core" (*Jude* 11), for the protest of Jorah, Dathan, and Abiram against Moses and Aaron, "Ye take too much upon you, seeing all the congregation are holy, and the Lord is among them; wherefore then lift ye up yourselves above the congregation of the Lord?" expresses exactly the idea underlying the title "Brethren" – absolute Equality.

Finally: Rome's dread weapon of excommunication once more assumed all the terrors of the Middle Ages and was as ruthlessly applied. To those who really believed that the little assemblies of "Brethren" were **The Church**, the Body of Christ, excommunication or cutting off from "fellowship" was a terrible calamity. The Reformed Churches of all embodied what they considered fundamental articles of faith in creeds or confessions of faith, and so long as a preacher did not violate any of these fundamentals he was allowed full liberty in expounding the Scriptures as he was led of the Spirit. But all these creeds were anathema to the Brethren. They had therefore no standard to determine what was fundamental and what was not. The Churches had some kind of ruling body regularly constituted which could determine questions of doctrine and form a court of appeal in the event of any member being unjustly dealt with in the congregation to which he belonged, as the Jerusalem Council in the Apostolic Church settled the question of circumcision, but such a Council as the Apostles held was contrary to the "Brethren" ideas of "Liberty, Equality, Fraternity." Each little "Assembly" was therefore a law unto itself. And as there was no ministry to govern according to fixed laws, those in each assembly who loved to have the pre-eminence lorded it over God's heritage, ruling them with a rod of iron. The result was a riot of wrangling and hair-splitting over points of doctrine or interpretation, followed by excommunications to right and left, seldom if ever elsewhere witnessed in the history of the Church. Ironside's History from start to finish is such a melancholy record as could scarcely be equalled in Christian annals, filled with pictures of little "assemblies like Soviets" excommunicating other "assemblies" or individuals. There was no appeal, no higher court. The only and natural reply that an assembly could give when excommunicated was to return the compliment. Time will not allow me to go into the case of Newton of Plymouth, of whom Ironside writes:

> "The late venerable man of God, Mr. Henry Varley, well-known as an evangelist and Bible teacher in Europe, America, and Australia, said to me on one occasion: 'If I were asked to name the godliest man I have ever known, I should unhesitatingly say, Benjamin Willis Newton.'[33] He described him as tall and of patriarchal bearing with the calm of heaven on his brow and the law of kindness on his lips. His intimate associates loved him devotedly and listened with rapt attention to his expositions."

Newton's preaching drew together what was the largest congregation in the pastoral work of the Brethren movement – so large that he was compelled to devote his whole time to the pastoral work, and so became a mere "hireling" according to Brethren views. He recognized the Scriptural injunction to ordain elders and deacons in each assembly – another grave fault. He even recognized that there were Christians in the "denominations" and was willing to have fellowship with them – an unpardonable sin in Brethren eyes, as his assembly thus ceased to claim to be **The Church**, the **whole** Body of

Christ in Plymouth, and became on its admission a mere branch or "sect" of the Church; this is what Brethren called "Sectarianism," the opposite of the ordinary dictionary meaning of that word. He unfortunately fell into the usual Brethren snare of injudicious speculations about the person and work of Christ, seeking, like many of them, to be wise above what is written: a plague has caused continual doctrinal controversies between Brethren leaders, and made charges of "heresy" fly thick and fast all through the movement. The excommunication of this eminent saint split the whole movement in two. Ironside says: "In the minds of many he is to this day the very incarnation of iniquitous teaching," which would alone justify the words of Dr. John Kennedy of Dingwall, that prince of Scottish preachers, who described Brethrenism as "broad in its creedlessness, narrow in its sectarianism, and lofty in its self-conceit."

But I must give one more sample of this spirit which shines out of page upon page of Ironside's story; and with this we must leave Cronin, the founder of the movement. In his old age, he came to reap the fruits of the system he had sown. In the Brethren assembly at Ryde there was a member who had married his deceased wife's sister. This was the same degree of relationship as the marriage of Herod to his brother's wife, which John Baptist declared unlawful, and owing to which he became a martyr. All churches, both Romish and Protestant, were agreed that it was unlawful, and it was also contrary to the law of England. This member had gone across to France, where since the Revolution many Bible laws had been set aside, and got married there. He had enough influence in the Brethren assembly to retain his "fellowship" in it, an unhallowed fellowship which soon brought the assembly to a condition which Mr. Darby emphatically describes as "rotten." It happened that an Anglican clergyman in

Ryde, a personal friend of Cronin's, wished to join the Brethren movement with his whole congregation. They had already withdrawn from the Anglican Church, but the rules of the Brethren required that the "rotten" assembly be recognized as **The Church** of Christ in Ryde and that this other congregation be dissolved and all apply as individuals for admission to the "rotten" assembly. Knowing the condition of that assembly, they refused to do this, and began to "break bread" as a separate assembly. Dr. Cronin visited Ryde and, after trying in vain to help the "rotten" assembly to cleanse themselves, he notified them that he was perfectly free to break bread with the new company which he did; an action that was looked upon as Ironside adds: "as a fearful sin in the eyes of those who put the new game above the souls of saints."

I must finish the story in the words of Ironside:

"Upon the aged doctor's return to his home assembly at Kennington he learned that his act had been construed by many as a definite over-attack on 'the ground of the one body.' Kennington, it was said, was one body with the rotten assembly at Ryde. It could not be one body with the new gathering, however godly and fragrant with Christian love and devotion.

But many saw otherwise and for about six months it was impossible to get concerted action at Kennington. Finally the patriarchal offender was excommunicated and for months sat back with the tears streaming down his face as his brethren remembered the Lord, and he, the first of them all was in the place of the immoral man or, the blasphemer. Finally he promised that, although unable to confess his act as sin, he would not offend in the same way again out of deference to the conscience of his brethren; but still he was kept under the ban. Is it any wonder that some critic said of the Brethren that they are 'people who are very particular about breaking bread, but very careless about breaking hearts?'"[34]

Poor Cronin! According to his own teaching, the assembly at Ryde who shielded the incestuous person and kept him in their fellowship, and his own assembly who became partakers in their guilt, were "the Body of Christ," **The Church**! If the Rapture were now to take place, they would be caught up, and he, having been cast out of the Church, would be left behind! No wonder he wept! It is a dangerous thing to be too logical. If we start out from false premises: the force of logic may lead us to most absurd conclusions. As if the usurper Diotrephes had power over the saints who befriended the Apostle John, to separate them from the Body of Christ, because he "cast them out of the Church" (III *John* 8, 9, 10). But if "the Church" which John there mentions was the body of Christ, as Rome and the Brethren maintain it always is, then Diotrephes had that power. Which is absurd!

It would be a weariness to follow all the divisions and excommunications, the charges and countercharges, which resulted from the expulsion of Dr. Cronin.

> "At Ramsgate a majority party, led by a fiery zealot, Mr. Jull, proceeded to excommunicate the entire Kennington Meeting for its dilatoriness in dealing with the 'wicked old doctor.'
>
> Because the minority refused to go with them in this hasty action they disowned them in like manner and went

out to start a new meeting 'on divine ground.' The majority met in Guildford Hall and the minority at Abbott's Hill, and these two names were destined to become well-known in the months and years that followed. Owing to an oversight about procuring the key to the Hall, the Abbott's Hillers did not get in to the breaking of bread the first Lord's Day after the division and so were later considered off church ground altogether. This is an important point to bear in mind in view of what happened in Montreal a few years later . . ."

Could anything be more grotesque and ridiculous? The fact that the incestuous person had been retained in fellowship was considered a mild offence in comparison with Cronin's crime in having fellowship with an assembly of Christians who were outside "the body of Christ." But to put the fool's cap on the whole proceedings; this little body in Ramsgate who refused to join in condemning Cronin were considered outside the "Body of Christ" because they had forgotten to get the key to their hall in time to "break bread" on the Lord's Day!

"Mr. Darby, now in his 81st year and a very sick man, pleaded vainly that no ultra severe measures be taken and declared that if questions like these were made tests of fellowship, he would not go with such wickedness."[35]

Yes, **vainly**. Dr. Cronin was out, and he was out **to stay out**. The London meeting with which Darby was connected was split in the same way in spite of Darby's pleadings, and its leader, William Kelly, a man of whom Spurgeon said that he had "a mind for universe narrowed by Darbyism," was also "cast out." Such was the beginning of similar splits all over the country. The celebrated George Muller of

Bristol was excommunicated because he differed from Darby on some points of doctrine so fine that most of you would not even understand what it was all about. And so it went on, till finally there were in almost every city two or more rival "assemblies" of Brethren, each claiming to be **the** church of Christ, and refusing to have any fellowship – not only with all the other churches – but also with each other.

Here was Satan's chosen method of breaking down the strong bulwark of evangelical religion, the "united front" which our Reforming forefathers had established against Rome, and under which the Protestant Churches had carried the Gospel to every corner of the globe.

1. Tractarianism was to awaken sympathy for Rome, and to eliminate the distinction between the Church of England and Rome by clandestinely introducing Romish practices into the Anglican services, so as to make it appear that the Churches of England and Rome were to all intents and purposes, one.
2. Brethrenism was to weaken the resistance to Rome by enticing the most spiritually-minded members to withdraw their support from the Protestant Churches to turn aside and waste their energies in vain jangling: obliterating as far as possible the distinction between the evangelical churches and Rome and falsely applying to the evangelical churches the warning which the Lord gave in regard to the idolatries of Babylon:

"Come out from among them and be ye separate."

And the very doctrine which the Tractarians were to use to awaken sympathy for Rome, the Brethren were to acclaim as a Divine Revelation placing them on a pedestal above all the saints of past ages, and above all the Protestant Churches in particular.

That Doctrine was the future individual personal Antichrist to appear after the Rapture of the Saints!

THE HOUR AND THE MAN

Let us glance at the man whom Brethrenism venerates as the revealer of this wonderful secret. J. N. Darby[36] came of a good Irish family, was educated for the bar, took high honours at the Dublin University, then turned aside, to his father's disgust, and became an Anglican curate. A brother of Cardinal Newman,[37] who became very intimate with him, thus describes his first impression of him:

> ". . . a most remarkable man, who rapidly gained an immense sway over me. His bodily presence was indeed 'weak.' A fallen cheek, a blood-shot eye, crippled limbs resting on crutches, a seldom shaven beard, a shabby suit of a clothes, and a generally neglected person, drew at first pity, with wonder to see such a figure in a drawing room."[38]

He had all the hallmarks of the religious zealot, and the description reminds one forcibly of the appearance of Ignatius Loyola after he had seen in a trance a vision of the Virgin Mary and had dedicated himself to founding the "Society of Jesus." Ironside says:

> "For a time he had hopefully followed the will-o-the-wisp of Tractarianism, and as a high churchman, he looked with a bigoted youth's disdain upon all other professing Christians, 'hoping they might find grace through the uncovenanted mercies of God,' but fearful that they were living and dying 'without benefit of clergy.'"[39]

This statement is illuminating. Ironside may seem to be a little out in the use of the word "Tractarianism," for he is referring to a period prior to 1827, the year in which Darby became definitely identified with Cronin's meeting in Dublin, and the Tractarian movement, according to Newman, was only founded in 1833. But the spirit of that movement was already abroad in the land, and although we are obliged to Ironside for the information, it would not have taken a great deal of discernment to guess that that spirit had taken a strong hold on Darby before ever he met Cronin. Brethrenism, in fact, was rocked in the cradle of Tractarianism, and if we had been looking for words in which to describe the attitude of Darby and all his followers towards all the other professing Christians we could not have any more suitably chosen than these of Ironside's.

Newman gives us another interesting sidelight:

"He had practically given up all reading but the Bible; and no small part of his movement soon took the form of dissuasion from all other voluntary study. In fact, I had myself more and more concentrated my religious reading on this one book: still I could not help feeling the value of a cultivated mind. Against this my new eccentric friend (having himself enjoyed no mean advantages of cultivation) directed his keenest attacks. I remember once saying to him: 'To desire to be rich is absurd: but if I were a father of children, I should wish to be rich enough to secure them a good education.' He replied: 'If I had children, I would as soon see them break stones on the road as do anything else, if only I could secure to them the Gospel and the grace of God.' I was unable to say Amen! But I admired his unflinching consistency, for now, as always, all he said was based on texts aptly quoted and logically enforced."[40]

You will say these are the words of a real fanatic. No man with a well-balanced mind would want to see his children breaking stones on the road if he could secure for them a good education with all the advantages it would bring them in their life's work. Having an education that would relieve them of life's drudgery would have no necessary bearing on their having or not having "the Gospel and the grace of God." In fact the education would enlarge their opportunities and usefulness in the Gospel.

But we do not see the true significance of Darby's revolt against general reading and study if we look at it only as the fanaticism of the man. There was method in the madness of the monks who laid down the principle that **ignorance is the mother of devotion**. There is a kind of pietism which thrives in a hotbed of ignorance, and like a mushroom will flourish in a darkness that may be felt. It is of a subjective and emotional nature, akin to auto-suggestion, easily captivated by any wind of doctrine with an emotional appeal, and averse to being trammelled by the cold facts of history or experience. Romanism, Anglo-Catholicism, and Brethrenism alike breed this kind of pietism in abundance. Rome protects it by placing all kinds of "dangerous" books (including the Bible) on the "Index." There was a logical necessity forcing both Anglo-Catholicism and Brethrenism to do the same, and Darby – or the spirit whose tool he was – was keen enough to see it. Ignorance of Church history was essential to the success of these movements. Men who knew the career of the Popes over centuries, their lewdness, blasphemies, cruelties, the millions of the saints of God whose blood they had shed, could not accept a puppet Antichrist of the future and call his reign of a few years "the great Tribulation." Men who had studied the contendings of the noble army of martyrs, and read the soul-satisfying expositions of Scripture by the Puritans, could not accept the necessity of "coming out from among" the followers of these saints and martyrs in order to join **The Church**, the Body of Christ. Those who were to be swept into this movement **must** be kept ignorant of the Church's whole past history. Mary Baker Eddy and others who have started a new brand of faith at variance with the contendings of the saints in the past, have seen this same necessity and prohibited their followers as far as possible from reading any other religious works but their own.

Some of you will find it hard to believe that "no small part of (Darby's) movement soon took the form of dissuasion from all other voluntary study." Darby was quite a writer himself, and his followers have turned out a vast quantity of tracts and other Christian literature. Surely he did not want people to refrain from reading his own writings! Of course not! The little bookshelf which every Christian home in Britain, no matter how poor, possessed at that time, contained as a rule Foxe's *Book of Martyrs*, *The Great Cloud of Witnesses*, and some of the writings of lives of the Reformers and Puritans. It was to consign these to oblivion that Darby's "dissuasion from all other voluntary study" was directed. But an even surer way of displacing them was to supply other reading material to take their place. The Tractarian Movement was so called on account of the "Tracts" of one man, Newman. But the real Tractarian Movement was Brethrenism, whose writers were legion. The objective of the two was the same: **not** to bring the Gospel to the unsaved (that is a secondary subject which is never allowed to interfere with the "Breaking of Bread" Meeting which is the kernel of the movement) **but** to entice out of the Churches those who were already followers of Christ. These, being under the care of their own pastors, could not be reached by preaching: the new doctrine must be slipped under their notice otherwise, and tracts and other religious literature were the most effective method. Here was "a tree to be desired to make one wise," the foretelling of future events which Christians could never have discovered for themselves by the most diligent study of the Bible, for the simple reason that they were not in the Bible. This detailed story of the coming Antichrist and all that he was to do, had all the subtle attraction of clairvoyancy or crystal-gazing. It enabled people to read between the lines of their Bible many things that their own ministers had never discovered, and so to become wise, very wise, above that which is written. It placed them on a pedestal from which they could look down with disdain on the very pastors who had led them to Christ. Well might the godly Dr. Kennedy refer to Brethrenism as "the slimiest of all isms." Not only is this new theory spread in tracts and magazines; it is dressed up in the form of novels: and in the Scofield Bible, the most subtle propaganda of all, the whole theory is incorporated in notes on the text of Scripture, in such a way that many simple souls read the notes as if they were a part of the Inspired Word of God. The Bible thus acquires a new meaning to them. They find in it new doctrines, of which their fathers never dreamt. Is it not because they are accepting the teaching of new gods, whom their fathers knew not?

Darby and the "Secret Rapture"

I have left to the last the crucial question of all – Was the "Secret Rapture of the Saints" given as a special revelation of the Holy Spirit to Darby, and through him to the Brethren Movement or did Darby simply borrow it from Irving, and through him from Lacunza, the Jesuit? In other words:

Did the Secret Rapture teaching originate with the Holy Spirit, or with the Jesuits?

Ironside is a believer in the "Secret Rapture." Let us read very carefully what he has to say on this point:

"A meeting began in London in the same year (1833), through a brother that Mr. Darby met while in Oxford. Some little time before this, a group of earnest Christians had been meeting in the castle of Lady Powerscourt[41] for the study of prophecy. To these meetings Mr. Darby and Mr. Bellett were invited. Here also they met George V. Wigram, who was to become one of Mr. Darby's most earnest collaborators in after years. At these meetings a chairman was chosen, and he indicated who should speak on the subject under discussion.

It became soon evident that Mr. Darby's enlightenment on prophetic themes was considerably in advance of most of the others, but the meetings were real conferences, the forerunners of the Bible readings so common in Brethren meetings, except that in such meetings a chairman is dispensed with. Many clergymen attended, and quite a few who were linked with the Irvingites, thus giving rise to the erroneous impression that the Brethren Movement was more or less linked with the 'Catholic Apostolic Church.' These Irvingites, however, soon dropped out, because the teaching was so contrary to what they held."[42]

"It was in these meetings that the precious truth of the rapture of the Church was brought to light; that is, the coming of the Lord in the air to take away His Church before the great tribulation should begin on earth. The views brought out at Powerscourt Castle not only largely formed the views of Brethren elsewhere, but as years went on obtained wide publication in denominational circles, chiefly through the writings of such men as Darby, Bellet, Newton, S. P. Tregelles, Andrew Jukes, Wigram, and after 1845 William Kelly, whose name was then linked with the movement; C. H. Mackintosh, Charles Stanley, J. B. Stoney and others."[43]

Now just what does Ironside tell us? He **does not** say that it was Darby who first announced the "Secret Rapture," though he obviously intends to convey that impression, and that is as far as any Futurist who is not a very rash one will venture to go. But Ironside is writing nearly a century after the event. Let us hear a witness who lived through this period. Dr. Tregelles,[44] the well-known Greek scholar and editor of the Greek New Testament, was a member of Mr. Newman's flock in Plymouth, and accepted the Futurist theory. You will notice that his name is included by Ironside in his list of those who helped to spread the "Secret Rapture" theory. He was probably the most learned man that has ever adorned the ranks of Brethrenism, and his name would be an asset to any cause. He may have been carried away with the new teaching for a time – long enough for Ironside to claim his name for it – but when he learned the facts of its origin he gave a clear ringing testimony against it. Here is his verdict:

> "I am not aware that there was any definite teaching that there would be a secret rapture of the Church at a secret coming, until this was given forth as an utterance in Mr. Irving's church, from what was there received as being the Voice of the Spirit. But whether anyone ever asserted

such a thing or not, it was from that supposed revelation that the modern doctrine and the modern phraseology arose. It came not from Holy Scripture, but from that which falsely pretended to be the Spirit of God."

"To the testimony of Dr. Tregelles is added that of Mr. Robert Baxter, the principal actor in the Irving scandals," says Cachemaille,[45] who was able to refer to Baxter's *Narrative of the Facts.*

With this apparently conflicting evidence before us, what conclusions may we safely draw?

We must assume that Ironside was ignorant of this testimony of Dr. Tregelles otherwise he could not honestly have included the name of Tregelles as he does among the supporters of the theory.

We may assume also, that Tregelles was ignorant of Irving's work in translating Lacunza, or at least had never examined this translation for himself, as his keen mind would at once have detected the connection between it and Irving's other vagaries, and in particular he would have discovered and pointed out that the origin of the "Secret Rapture" was in the work of the Jesuit.

When Newton and his flock were cast out of the ranks of Brethrenism, Dr. Tregelles was of course excommunicated along with the rest. Among the many doctrinal differences between Darby and Newton, we can be sure that Tregelles' exposure of the "Secret Rapture," though not mentioned by Ironside, would be accounted not the least serious.

Let us now analyse the information Ironside has given, and see what it contains.

"It was in these meetings that the precious truth of the rapture of the Church was brought to light."[46]

In this statement Ironside is guilty of the serious misuse of words common among the Brethren: he speaks of "the rapture" when he means "the secret rapture," an entirely different thing. "The Rapture" or the taking up of the Church was first "brought to light" by Paul in I *Thessalonians*, the very earliest of his epistles, and was cherished by the saints as part of the blessed hope of Christ's glorious appearing for about eighteen centuries before the Powerscourt meetings. But the **Secret** "rapture" was (as we may correctly infer from Ironside) unknown to either Paul or any of the apostles or saints or martyrs, being only "brought to light" (so far as he knows) at these meetings.

Were the Powerscourt meetings started for the express purpose of "bringing to light" the "secret rapture?" The theory had been in print for six years in Irving's **translation** of Lacunza. It had been preached by Irving in his own church, and was regarded as one of the distinctive tenets of his own Irvingite sect. But the spirit manifestations in connection with his preaching of the new doctrine had put the Christian public on their guard, so that it took him six years to dispose of the first edition of his translation. Then, in this fateful 1833, in which Newman floated the Tractarian Movement, appeared the cheap popular edition of Lacunza, and about the same time the Powerscourt meetings were opened "for the study of prophecy." Would it be a very wild guess to surmise that the anonymous editors of Lacunza were among the promoters of the Powerscourt meetings?

Here are one or two points to notice:

1. Darby and the other Brethren leaders, who as yet knew nothing of a "Secret Rapture" had nothing to do with organizing the meetings. They "were invited," and went apparently quite innocent of any previous knowledge of what was to be brought to light.

2. The Irvingites came to the meetings obsessed with the ideas of the "Secret Rapture" and the future of Antichrist, which they would naturally bring to light at the first opportunity.

The result proves the correctness of these conclusions. Ironside says the presence of these Irvingites at the Powerscourt meetings (though there is nothing to show that they were "Brethren" meetings at all) gave rise to the erroneous impression that the Brethren Movement was more or less linked with the 'Catholic Apostolic Church.' But the public do not form their "impression" on such slight grounds as Ironside would have us believe. No one would jump to the conclusion, merely because a series of special studies taken part in by members of his church were attended by some members of another church, that there is some link between his church and that other. The public would not pry into who was attending some semi-private meetings in Powerscourt Castle. But when Darby and the other Brethren leaders came out from these meetings and began zealously to publish all over the country some of the "precious truth," as Ironside calls it that had been first announced during the fanatical outbreak in Irving's church, the Christian public could come to only one conclusion, and who shall say that their impression was an erroneous one? The facts all pointed in the one direction.

Ironside hastens to point out that the Irvingites "soon dropped out, because the teaching was so contrary to what they held."[47] What teaching? Certainly not the teaching as to the "Secret Rapture" followed by the reign of Antichrist. It is probable, of course, that the Irvingites would maintain the position taken by Lacunza who as we have seen made concessions to the Protestant viewpoint so far as to allow that the Antichrist was not merely one individual, but a vast system under one official head; and that as the usurper of the prerogatives of Christ, the Antichrist would occupy the seat of the papacy. Darby and his followers, as the Brethren teachings show, were not satisfied with any such half-way house, but went right over to the undiluted teaching of the Jesuit school of Ribera as to an individual personal Antichrist. On this point there might be some disagreement, but it is not likely that it was this alone which caused the withdrawal of the Irvingites. Darby was keen on a belief of his own, which the Brethren lovingly refer to as "Dispensational Truth," but which Newton called "speculative nonsense." The Irvingites had a number of "revelations" equally speculative and equally nonsensical. It was not to be expected that either party would accept all the speculations of the other; and in a conflict of speculations the dogmatism of Darby made it a foregone conclusion that the Brethren leaders, though only there by invitation, would finally be left in possession of the field.

So much for the withdrawal of the Irvingites, of which much has been made by the Brethren by way of showing that they and the Irvingites had nothing in common. But whatever the differences between them – and they were neither few nor small – on the matter of the "Secret Rapture" they were

> "Two minds with but a single thought,
> Two hearts that beat as one."

Or to adopt a homely metaphor, Darby had swallowed the Irvingite bait, "hook, line and sinker": and on seeing this, it may have been policy on their part to retire and leave him free to spread the new doctrine in his own way, unhampered by the stigma that was attached to their sect.

It is now over a hundred years[48] since the Powerscourt Castle meetings, and in all that has been spoken and written on this subject in that time, no one appears to have been able to explain how a belief which was known to be a Jesuit invention and had for two-and-a-half centuries been confined to the Church of Rome, suddenly began to spread like wildfire among evangelical Christians. I believe that I have submitted satisfactory proof that this fire did not originate, as has been supposed, by spontaneous combustion at Powerscourt. Lacunza, alias "Rabbi Ben Ezra," was the mysterious "missing link" who has escaped notice right up until now. I have shown how by a subtle approach to the Reformers' position, and by being put on Rome's "Index," his work was gilded to gain the favour of Protestants; then, how the sugar-coated pill was thrust under the noses of the Protestant British, by being published in London; how Maitland and Irving fell into the trap; and finally how in 1833 the spreading of the new teaching was formally undertaken by Tractarianism on the one hand and Brethrenism on the other. At every stage the evidence is sufficient to satisfy any unbiased mind.

God in many marvellous ways brings good out of evil, if only we know how to appreciate and use His good gifts. In 1837, Rev. E. B. Elliott began his monumental *Horae Apocalypticae*, which he published in 1844, bringing together such a mass of evidence to prove from the pages of History that the Book of *Revelation* had up to date been fulfilled in all its minutest details, as is startling and overwhelming in all its force. No one can read it without standing in awe of the Divine Majesty, revealing before in sublime symbolism to the saints every event among the nations that was to affect the Church's welfare. The preparation of this inexhaustible storehouse of facts, which has confirmed the faith of so many in "the depth of the riches both of the wisdom and knowledge of God," was suggested to Elliott by the increasing prevalence among Christian men in our country of the futurist system of Apocalyptic interpretation – a system which involved the abandonment of the opinion held by all the chief fathers and doctors of our church, respecting the Roman Popes and Popedom as the great intended anti-Christian power of Scripture prophecy. We ought to thank God for over-ruling even the wiles of the Jesuits to bestow on the Church such a masterly vindication of "the faith once delivered to the saints."

Elliott was not the only Defender of the Faith. In 1839, there appeared the *Key to the Prophecies*, by Rev. David Simpson – a little volume which is now very rare. A well-known evangelist recently showed me a copy which he had picked up at the bookstall in the States for 25 cents, and said he would not sell it for a thousand dollars; he had learnt more about prophecy from that one little book than from all he ever read on the subject. Dr. Cumming of London had to leave his own church and take the Albert Hall, and even that was packed to hear his *Apocalyptic Sketches* which afterwards had a wide circulation, reviving the interest in the remarkable fulfilment of prophecy in history as brought out by Elliott. Even Darby's friend William Kelly, though a leader of the Futurist school, finally renounced many of their dogmas and accepted the Historical fulfilment of prophecy.

I have at times been confronted with an imposing array of names of Bible teachers – Gaebelein, Panton, Scofield, etc.,[49] who believe in the "secret rapture" and the Future Personal Antichrist. How can I dare to assert that these men are all wrong? I dare to go further than that. I will venture to assert that – **there is not a Bible Teacher nor anyone else living in the world today who has found a Secret Rapture in the Bible by his own independent study of the Bible itself.** These teachers all come to the Bible with cut-and-dried theories which they have learnt elsewhere, and twist and torture texts to fit the theory. If the spiritual pedigree of these Futurist Bible Teachers could be traced back, they would all be found to spring from one source – **Lacunza – the Jesuit.**

Be not deceived! God is not the Author of confusion. He has not given us the Book of *Revelation* to put our minds in a muddle, nor yet as a Happy Hunting Ground for our imagination. We should be very careful how we speculate or dogmatize about any prophecy that is as yet unfulfilled.[50] When a prophecy is fulfilled, then we can see and understand the meaning of every detail of the symbolism used, and what we know of this must be our main guide to the meaning of prophecies still in the future: the average Futurist cannot put his finger on a single prophecy in the Book of *Revelation* which has proved itself to him, by its actual fulfilment to be the Word of the Living God. I hope in this series of studies to show how verses and even whole chapters have been torn from their proper setting and twisted into the most fantastic shapes, to prove theories equally far-fetched: even after the prophecy had been fulfilled in the most exact detail. But in case any of you should miss the other lectures, I shall close with one word of advice.

Many even of our Futurist friends are constrained to admit that the world is **at this moment** hastening towards the great Battle[51] of Armageddon, mentioned in *Revelation* 16:16. The three unclean spirits like frogs (v. 13-14) have now been at work in the world for a whole century, and their deceptions are rapidly coming to a head in preparing the nations for battle against God Almighty. One of the results as might have been expected under the sway of these spirits of devils has been the rise of many antichrists of every shape and colour. Our Bible teachers have plenty of material to work on.

First Mussolini was the Antichrist; they were all sure of it. But Mussolini ordered the Bible to be taught in all schools in Italy, and our prophets grew a little less positive about him. Stalin, Hitler, and even Roosevelt, have shared the honour of being singled out as the Antichrist, or at least, his forerunner.

This is mere trifling with a solemn subject. If we are approaching the Battle of Armageddon, we are well on through chapter 16 of *Revelation*. But the career of Antichrist occurs in chapter 13, and no man has any authority or right to tear chapter 13 out of its place and thrust it into the middle of chapter 16.

A historian records the fact of History in chronologic order. He never leaves the natural order of events except for some reason which he makes clear to his readers; otherwise all would be confusion. God does not produce such confusion. He has given us a record of events that were to come to pass, that is, History Written Beforehand, for the guidance of the Church. It is divided into three great periods in which

God's judgments are foretold under the symbols of Seven Seals (clearly before the reign of Antichrist); and seven Vials (clearly after the reign of Antichrist). All the nations are now rushing their preparations for the last of these judgments;

"The seventh angel poured out his vial into the **air**."

Keep your eye on that word. John knew nothing of the horrors of war in the **air** as we know it will be. Radio, fighting and bombing airplanes, poison gas, disease germs, infrared rays – all the means for carrying on war in the air that can wipe out a whole population in a few hours or even minutes – such diabolical weapons of destruction were undreamed of by our own grandfathers, let alone the simple fishermen of Galilee. But John, seeing in his Vision the final crash that would bring the present system of civilization toppling in ruin, wrote nearly nineteen hundred years ago:

"The seventh angel poured out his vial into the **air**."

That is the Grand Climax, so far as God's judgments on this age are concerned. It not only brings down "the cities of the nations": it will bring suddenly to remembrance the career of Antichrist and the war which he made against the saints, which our Futurist Bible teachers[52] are so feverishly trying to help the world to forget. The Babylonish system of Antichrist, described by John in chapter 17, is still in existence, still "drunken with the blood of the saints," gloating over the "war" and massacre of the saints described in chapter 13. All that remains of Antichrist in the future is the final and complete destruction of his whole system, which though occupying the whole of chapters 17 and 18, is part of the immediate result of the pouring out of the Seventh Vial.

The "Rapture of the Saints" occurs in chapter 19, and nowhere else in the Book of *Revelation*. Don't be misled! John saw the saints who are already in heaven, (there have been saints and martyrs in heaven ever since Abel went home to glory); but there is but one "Rapture," and that will be when Christ shall come in the Glory of the Father with his Holy Angels.

---000---

Publishers' Note

Modern scholarship on the works of Isaac Newton has revealed his deep interest in theology and prophecy. For further study readers can refer to this website from which the following quotes are taken:

https://isaac-newton.org/statement-on-the-date-2060/

"On 22 February 2003, *The Daily Telegraph* (London, England) published a front-page story announcing Isaac Newton's prediction that the world would end in 2060."

"… Isaac Newton was not merely a "scientist," but also a theologian and a prophetic exegete …"

"For many, the revelation that Newton was a passionate believer who took biblical prophecy seriously came as something of a shock."

"Newton believed both in God and that the Bible was a revelation from God. He also believed that God was not bound by time as are humans, allowing Him to see the "end from the beginning." Thus, to use Newton's own words, he was convinced that "the holy Prophecies" of the Scripture are nothing else than "histories of things to come" (Yahuda MS 1.1, folio 16 recto)."

NOTES

1. Definitions of Historicist, Futurist and Praeterist; *Encyclopaedia Britannica*, 11th Edition, XXIII, 213c-iii & iv. *English New Testament,* Alford (1872); Vol. II, Part II, 348a, b, c. *Revelation of Jesus Christ,* (1966), J. F. Walvoord; pp. 17-22. *Halley's Bible Handbook,* 19th Edition; pp. 614-615.
2. RIBERA: Jesuit author of the Future Antichrist concept – *Old Fashioned Prophecy Magazine* Dec., 1965, p. 10. *Revelation of St John* (1644), Thomas Brightman (Ribera's Contemporary); pp. A-4, 181. 188. etc. *Ency. Brit* 11th Ed; XXIII, 213c. *Greek New Testament,* Alford (1866); IV, 248. *Horae Apocalypticae,* E. B. Elliott (1851); IV, 465. *The Beasts and the Little Horn,* G. S. Hitchcock (Roman Catholic); p. 7. (published 1911 by the Roman Catholic Truth Society). See comment p. 73.
3. *The Coming of Messiah in Glory and Majesty,* by Juan Josafat Ben Ezra; Dublin, 1833, Wm Curry Jun., & Co., pp. 10 & 11.
4. Ibid, p. 92.
5. Ibid, p. 113, 114.
6. Ibid, but could not locate page due to delicate condition of book.
7. *Encyc. Brit.,* 11th Edition; VII, 915-917.
8. *Prophetic Faith of Our Fathers,* Leroy Froom (1946); III. 303-324.
9. 1892 Edition, p. 98 et seq.
10. *Prophetic Faith,* Froom; II. 657. *History Unveiling Prophecy,* Guinness (1905); pp. 285-289.
11. See note 2.
12. *Historicism, Preterism, Futurism; What Are These?* E. P. Cachemaille (1929); p. 44.
13. Ibid.
14. *The Coming of Messiah,* but could not locate page due to delicate condition of book.
15. Ibid.
16. *Prophetic Faith,* Froom; III, 258. *Horae,* Elliott; IV, 554.
17. *History Unveiling Prophecy,* Guinness; pp. 281-295.
18. On page 48 of his *Apologia,* in reference to his close friendship with Froude, Cardinal Newman said, "He made me look with admiration towards the Church of Rome, and, in the same degree, to dislike the Reformation." *Everyman's Library.*
19. *Secret History of the Oxford Movement,* Walter Walsh (1899); 5th Edition, p. 1.
20. Pusey; Hater of Protestantism, eulogizer of Jesuitry and "frightened at calling Rome Antichrist." – Ibid, pp. 289-292. See Puseyism; Puseyite in *Webster's Twentieth Century Dictionary,* (1935).
21. Walsh's book is a thorough exposure of this hellish movement; see also *The Oxford Movement Exposed,* Rev. Thomas Houghton (1932).
22. Faber: famous writer of hymns "largely used in Protestant collections," who was converted to Romanism. He was already a Romanist for five years when he wrote *Faith of Our Fathers. Encyc. Brit.,* 11th Edition, X, 111-112. Another

music-coated Romanist pill that Protestants have long been swallowing is *Ave Maria – Hail Mary.* Just what is the matter with Protestants?
23. *Prophetic Faith,* Froom; III, 514-526: IV, 420-422. *Hist. Unv. Prophecy,* Guinness; p. 240. *Horae,* Elliott; IV, 552.
24. *The Coming of Messiah,* Ben Ezra, pp. 10 and 11.
25. Pusey, Keble, Newman and Froude mentioned as "chief leaders." *Oxford Movement Exposed,* Houghton, p. 8.
26. See note No. 3 reference; also p. 19 of note No. 27 reference – "the **voice**."
27. *The Prophetic Outlook Today,* E. P. Cachemaille (1918); p. 20.
28. Plymouth Brethren: *Encyc. Brit.,* 11th Edition, XXI, p. 864.
29. Or to modernize the thought – "Scratch a Futurist-Fundamentalist and you still draw Tractarian blood." My! My! How the Brethren have blossomed!
30. Written when Dr. Ironside was still alive.
31. *Prophetic Faith,* Froom; IV, p. 223, note 6.
32. *A Historical Sketch of the Brethren Movement,* Ironside, p. 10.
33. *Prophetic Faith,* Froom; IV, 1223-1225. Ironside, p. 23.
34. Ironside, pp. 84-85.
35. Ironside, p. 9.
36. *Prophetic Faith,* Froom; IV, 1223, 1225, 1226 and footnotes.
37. Francis William Newman: Ironside, p. 13.
38. Francis William Newman quotes: Ironside, p. 13.
39. Ironside, p. 13.
40. Francis William Newman quotes: Ironside, p. 14.
41. Powerscourt: *Prophetic Faith,* Froom; IV, 1223-1225 and footnotes.
42. Ironside, p. 23.
43. Ironside, p. 23.
44. Tregelles: *Prophetic Faith,* Froom; IV, 442, 1223 and 1225 note.
45. *The Prophetic Outlook Today,* E. P. Cachemaille; p. 19.
46. Ironside, p. 23.
47. Ironside, p. 23.
48. About 140 years at this printing.
49. **Plus** many names fearlessly mentioned in *Old Fashioned Prophecy Magazine* often, such as Seiss, Stearns, Pettingill, Panton, McBirnie, Winrod, Estep, Barnhouse, the Joneses, the Beirneses, Oliver Greene, Oral Roberts, Schiffner, Gilpin, John Douglas, Billy Graham, G. L. K. Smith, Wilber Smith, Oswald Smith, Noel Smith, V. Sears, Herbert Armstrong, Walvoord, and scores of big-name evangelists and thousands of lesser lights orating and prating false prophecy over pulpit tops and the airwaves *ad nauseam!*
50. The great sin of the Futurists! Of such is one named above, Oliver Greene, who broadcasts all over the world. Even at this writing he is teaching Revelation over the air, Futurist style, and hoodwinking thousands of trusting souls and placing them all in the ranks of the *deceived elect.* Of what use is *100% sound Gospel* when, with a flick of a finger and just one error in Prophecy, you sluice multitudes of saved Christians back into the Church of Rome? With that Romanized version of a prophecy, originally intended to scare Christians away from Rome, but which

now entices them back? (*Notice*: Oliver Greene's Gospel is our Gospel too! Our quarrel is not with his Gospel. No!).
51. Should be "war" according to Alford and the A.V.R. – *Revelation* 16:14 note. Some expositors with good reason, expound this "war" as beginning with World War I, *which never terminated in a peace*. The world is still in a state of war! This is sound logic and truth and we must therefore be in the midst of Armageddon and have been at least 56 years. It is no more "Future" than a lot of other "Future" things of the Futurists. The **big thing** certain to be future is our Lord's Second Coming **in one complete act** – not a **divided act** stipulated as "*a coming for*" and a later "*coming with*" His saints, as is popularly taught by the deceived elect Protestant Clergy today! The "Great Tribulation" is 99% behind us, friends, and our King is coming soon to end it, bringing our rewards with Him! – *Revelation* 22:12 and *Luke* 19:13.
52. The Futurist Prophetic Beagle is so busy sniffing at things *Future and Negative* that he fails to concern himself with the remarkable events of the *Present and Positive* which are the fulfilments of Apocalyptic Prophecy **now**. He has rammed his sniffer so deeply into the Future Jesuitic Mud that even his eyes and ears are buried in the Future, and "**having eyes he sees not and having ears he hears not.**"

Francisco Ribera was a doctor of theology from Spain who had studied the prophecies of the Bible. He wrote a 500 page commentary on the Book of *Revelation* entitled *In Sacrum Beati Ioannis Apostoli, & Evangelistiae Apocalypsin Commentarii*. The book was published around 1590. He said that the Antichrist was not an apostate church or anything like that but rather referred to one man who would be revealed prior to the return of Jesus. He said that the first three chapters of the Book of *Revelation* referred to Rome and the rest of the book was mostly about the three and one half year reign of the Antichrist-man.

He believed that up until the 6th seal the Book of *Revelation* is about pagan Rome but after that it is referring to an event that is in the future. This Antichrist would rebuild the temple in Jerusalem and would be received by the Jews. He would be the "little horn" referred to by the Book of *Daniel* (*Daniel* 7:8). Ribera said that there would be a time of apostasy ('falling away') from the true church prior to the future event of the Antichrist. For Ribera, the true church was the Roman Catholic Church and it is obviously implied that the Protestants are those apostates who fell away.

Barry G Carpenter,
20 August, 2018
Founder and dean of Mindanao Grace Seminary, Philippines.